Collins

# ALL ABOUT
# THE WORLD

Published by Collins
An imprint of HarperCollins*Publishers*
1 Robroyston Gate
Glasgow
G33 1JN

HarperCollins*Publishers*
Macken House,
39/40 Mayor Street Upper,
Dublin 1, D01 C9W8, Ireland

collins.co.uk

First published 2025

© HarperCollins*Publishers* 2025

Collins® is a registered trademark of HarperCollins*Publishers* Ltd.

Text by: Joseph Barnes
'Ask an expert' contribution by: Gabrielle Aisya

Publisher: Beth Rogers
Project leader: Rachel Allegro
Cover and interior design: James Hunter & Rachel Allegro
Editorial: Tracey Cowell & Louise Robb
Production: Ilaria Rovera

Photo credits
All photos © Shutterstock, except: p.14(t): Ken Howard / Alamy; p.14(b): Adrian Cabello / Alamy; p.15(t): PA Images / Alamy; p.16(b): Osborne Hollis / Alamy; p.17(t): Sipa US / Alamy; p.17(b): Emma Wood / Alamy; p.19(c): Dmitriy Shironosov / Alamy; p.24(b): Photostock-Israel/Science Photo Library; p.26(br): CGIAR Platform for Big Data in Agriculture / CC by 3.0; p.32: FM Archive / Alamy; p.36: Jaime Franch Travel Photo / Alamy, p.37(br): Album / Alamy; p.40(b): Mark Garlick/Science Photo Library; p.41(t): Gwen Shockey/Science Photo Library; p.43(b): Mikkel Juul Jensen / Science Photo Library; p.60(b): Karsten Schneider/Science Photo Library; p.61(tr): Album / Alamy; p.63(t): Science History Images / Alamy; p.73(b): Planet Labs / CC by 4.0; p.77(t): Ali Damouh/Science Photo Library; p.82(b): Jim West / Alamy; p.85(c): Science History Images / Alamy

All rights reserved. No part of this publication may be reproduced, stored in a retrieval system, or transmitted, in any form or by any means, electronic, mechanical, photocopying, recording or otherwise without the prior permission in writing of the publisher and copyright owners.

Without limiting the author's and publisher's exclusive rights, any unauthorised use of this publication to train generative artificial intelligence (AI) technologies is expressly prohibited. HarperCollins also exercise their rights under Article 4(3) of the Digital Single Market Directive 2019/790 and expressly reserve this publication from the text and data mining exception.

The contents of this publication are believed correct at the time of printing. Every care has been taken in the preparation of this book. However, the publisher can accept no responsiblity for errors or omissions, changes in detail given or for any expense or loss thereby caused.

A catalogue record for this book is available from the British Library.

ISBN 9780008737566

Printed by LEGO, Italy.

10 9 8 7 6 5 4 3 2 1

This book is produced from independently certified FSC™ paper to ensure responsible forest management. For more information visit: www.harpercollins.co.uk/green

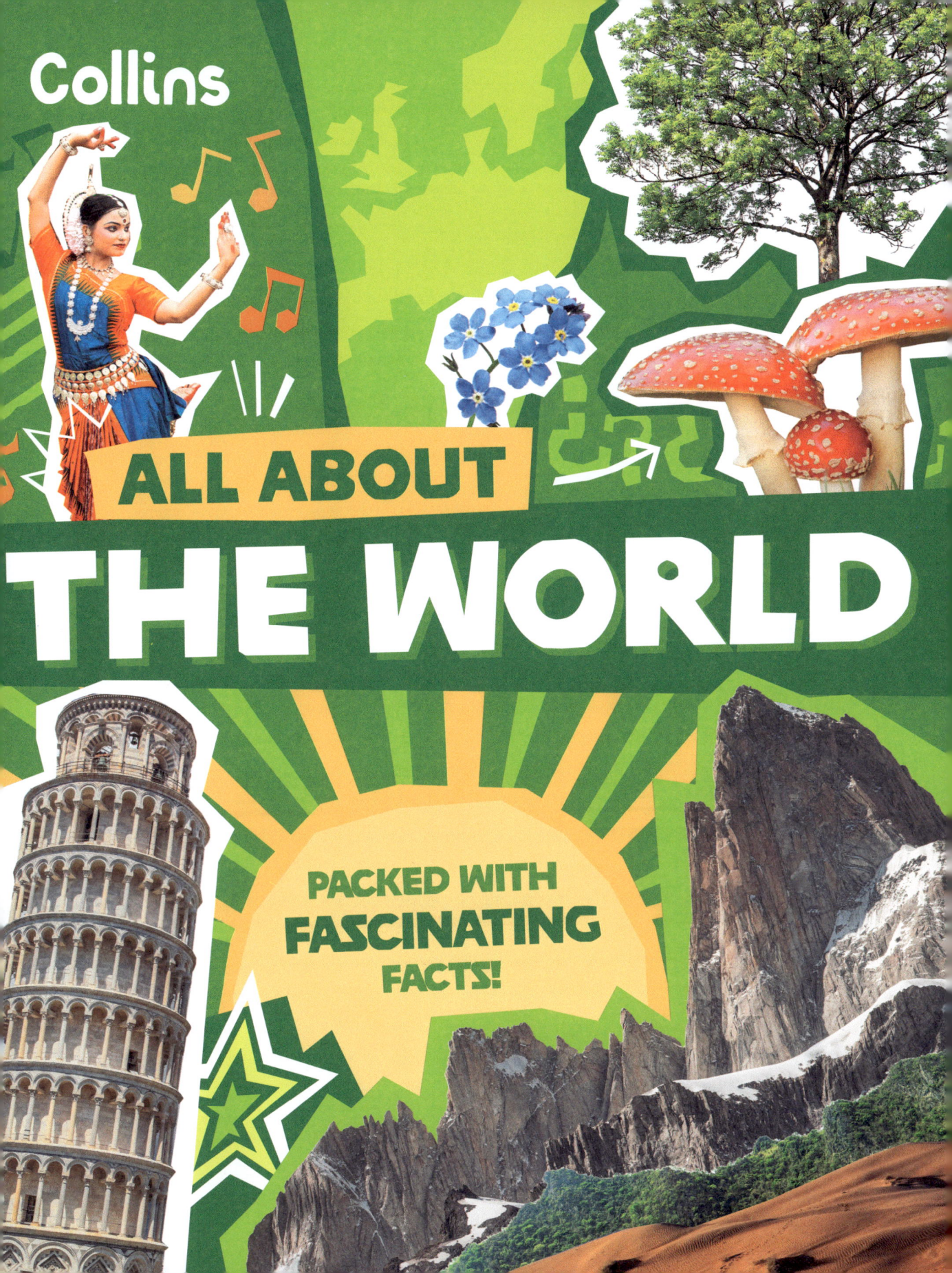

# CONTENTS

Our world .................................. 8
Super stats: Cities ................. 10
Culture ...................................... 12
Art and literature ................... 14
Sport ......................................... 16
Music and dance ................... 18
Religions and festivals ......... 20
Languages ............................... 22
Money ....................................... 24
Super stats: Food .................. 26

Name that...
    World flag ........................... 28
Earth's beginnings ................ 30
Inside Earth ............................ 32
Mountains ............................... 34
Volcanoes ................................ 36
Earthquakes ............................ 38
Tsunamis .................................. 40
Fossils ....................................... 42
Rock ........................................... 44
Minerals .................................... 46
Quiz yourself on...
    Planet Earth ........................ 48

| | |
|---|---|
| Water | 50 |
| Ice | 52 |
| Rivers | 54 |
| Super stats: Lakes | 56 |
| Oceans | 58 |
| Deep sea | 60 |
| Atmosphere | 62 |
| Super stats: Weather | 64 |
| Weathering and erosion | 66 |
| Deserts | 68 |
| Forests | 70 |
| Trees | 72 |
| Plants | 74 |
| Name that… Flower | 76 |
| Fungi | 78 |
| Climate change | 80 |
| Ask an expert about… Marine conservation | 82 |
| Protecting our planet | 84 |
| Quiz yourself on… Our wonderful world | 86 |
| Answers | 88 |
| Glossary | 90 |
| Index | 94 |

# Wonderful world

Planet Earth is our home, but many of us have only seen an incredibly small part of it. From dry and deadly deserts to marvellous and massive mountains, the world is full of wonders...

# OUR WORLD

There are almost 200 countries in the world today and there are seven different continents. A country is an area that is controlled by a single government, and a continent is a large geographical region that's usually made up of lots of countries.

**FASCINATING FACT**

Not everywhere on Earth is on a continent – for example, the North Pole isn't considered to be part of a country as it sits on drifting sea ice!

North America is the third largest continent. It stretches from the cold polar regions in the north down to the warm tropical areas of Florida in the south.

South America is the fourth largest continent and is made up of 12 countries.

Antarctica is the coldest of the continents, and it is the fifth largest. Antarctica is the only continent that is not divided into countries.

North America

South America

Antarctica

# Mapping the world

The Earth is shaped like a giant ball, and a model of this is called a globe. Maps like this one are called 'map projections'. They are attempts by map makers (cartographers) to show the curved surface of the Earth on a flat surface.

**FASCINATING FACT**

Zealandia is a microcontinent that broke off from Australia around 80–100 million years ago. It is mostly under the water, beneath the South Pacific Ocean. About 6% of Zealandia pokes above the surface to form the islands of New Zealand and New Caledonia.

Europe is the second smallest continent. It has over 40 countries.

Asia is the largest continent, and covers around 30% of the Earth's land area.

Oceania is the smallest continent, and is also home to some of the smallest countries in the world.

Africa is the second largest continent and has the most countries – today there are 54.

Europe

Asia

Africa

Oceania

# Super Stats

# CITIES

Most people live in a village, town or city. Villages are small communities in the countryside. Towns are bigger than villages and have more homes, shops, schools and things people need in everyday life. Cities are very large towns and are the biggest settlements – they often have millions of people living in them.

## Top 5 biggest cities (by area)

1. New York city, USA
2. Boston-Providence, USA
3. Tokyo-Yokohama, Japan
4. Atlanta, USA
5. Chicago, USA

New York city

**FASCINATING FACT**

Megacities are cities with more than 10 million people living in them.

## Top 5 biggest cities (by population)

1. Tokyo, Japan: 37.4 million people
2. Delhi, India: 29.3 million people
3. Shanghai, China: 26.3 million people
4. São Paulo, Brazil: 21.8 million people
5. Mexico City, Mexico: 21.6 million people

Tokyo

# Smallest city

Vatican City in Rome is both the smallest city and the smallest country in the world. It is less than half of a square kilometre and has a population of around 800.

# Highest cities

The neighbouring cities El Alto and La Paz in Bolivia are the highest cities in the world. El Alto is 4,061 metres above sea level, and nearby La Paz is 3,640 metres above sea level. Because of this, the air is much thinner, so visitors need time to get used to breathing the thin air.

La Paz

# Hottest and coldest cities

Yakutsk

The coldest city in the world is Yakutsk in Russia. It can drop to a super-chilly -42°C in winter, and has less than four hours of sunlight at this time of year. The hottest city in the world in 2024 was Doha in Qatar, where the average temperature was a scorching 41°C.

# Capital cities

A capital city is usually where a country's government is located. There are currently 195 official capitals in the world. Not all countries have a capital city, though: for example, Monaco, Vatican City and Singapore are city states, so don't have a separate capital.

# Petra, Jordan

Petra is an ancient city that was built into the pink sandstone of the desert in Jordan over 2,000 years ago. At that time, it was home to around 30,000 people. Today it is one of the seven wonders of the world.

# CULTURE

Culture is made up of many different things: language, history, gender, age, celebrations, beliefs, nationality, food, art, music, clothing... We are all part of a culture and it gives us a feeling of belonging. The things we share give us our cultural identity.

## Multicultural

Many people feel they are part of more than one culture. For example, you could have grandparents from Italy and live in Wales, so you could be a part of both Welsh and Italian culture. Many countries are multicultural as people often move all around the world.

## Where you live

The place where you live and grow up will have a big influence on your cultural identity, as you learn from what you see around you every day. Your family might also influence your religious beliefs or the kinds of books and music you like.

**FASCINATING FACT**

Scientists who study culture are called anthropologists. By studying lots of different cultures around the world they can see how culture develops, how the place in which people live affects their culture, and the things that all cultures share but do a little differently.

## Cave paintings

Cave paintings are evidence of very early culture. They show how people thought, how they lived, and how they communicated and expressed themselves thousands of years ago. Some of the oldest cave paintings in the world are on the island of Sulawesi in Indonesia.

## Exploring other cultures

You can learn about other cultures through people who live near you or by travelling to other places. You'll find you have many shared experiences with people from other cultures, and accepting any differences is likely to have a positive effect on how you live your life.

## Art, music and sport

The things you do can also shape your cultural identity. For example, people might see themselves as skateboarders, artists, musicians or mountaineers. All of these activities and interests have their own way of life and give people a community and sense of belonging.

# ART AND LITERATURE

Humans have always had a desire to be creative, express thoughts, ideas and emotions, and tell stories. Books, paintings, poems, sculptures and many more forms of art and literature are how we do it.

'Number 1, 1950' by Jackson Pollock

## Abstract art

Some paintings are of people or of natural scenery. Abstract art uses colour, shape and texture to represent something that we wouldn't see in our world. The artist often tries to explore ideas or create an atmosphere with their art. One of the most famous abstract artists was Jackson Pollock, who used a 'drip technique' to create his paintings.

## Street art

Some artists choose to use spray paints and create art around the city they live in – sometimes without permission! Bristol is famous for its street art and hosts a festival called Upfest where artists are invited to paint large murals on the sides of buildings.

## Installations

An art installation is where an artist transforms a space. The space and the objects in it are all part of the artwork for the viewer to enter and interact with.

## Fiction and non-fiction

Literature – or written texts – fall into two main categories: fiction and non-fiction. Fiction is when a story and the characters in it are made up, though it can often be set in a real-life place. Non-fiction is a book about facts, people and actual things happening in the world.

## Printing press

In 1440 Johannes Gutenberg invented the printing press. It used moveable metal letters that were covered in ink to print text onto paper. Before the invention of the printing press, books were copied out by hand!

# SPORT

A sport is a physical activity that requires skill or technique. Some sports are competitions or games, some are creative, some are just for fun. Some are about testing how fit you are. Sports can be team-based or you can do them on your own.

## Team sports

Team sports, like football, cricket and rugby, are some of the most popular sports in the world. Road cycling races, running relay races and Formula One motor races are also well-known team sports.

## Individual sports

There are lots of games and competitions where people compete on their own against other individuals, like in marathon running, tennis and golf. Gymnastics is an artistic sport where the athletes are judged on the difficulty of their moves and how well they do them. In creative sports like surfing, rock climbing and snowboarding, people sometimes compete against each other but often they do them just to challenge themselves or simply to have fun.

## Adaptive and disability sports

Many sports can be adapted to meet the needs of different people. The Paralympics is one of the biggest international events for athletes with disabilities, where many of the sports from the Olympics are adapted to meet the needs of participants. Popular events include goalball, boccia and wheelchair rugby, which is also known as 'Murderball'!

Murderball

## Age doesn't matter

Age isn't important if you've got the skills for a sport! At the 2024 Paris Olympics, the British skateboarding team consisted of Sky Brown and Lola Tambling, who were both teenagers, and Andy Macdonald, who was 51 years old at the time.

## Alternative sports

In 1985, the first World Bog Snorkelling Championship was held in Wales. Competitors wear facemasks and snorkels and must swim two lengths of the bog (110 metres). In 2005, the World Mountain Bike Bog Snorkelling Championship began, where participants attempt to ride an adapted mountain bike through the trench twice, getting covered head to toe in muddy bog water!

# MUSIC AND DANCE

Music and dance often go hand in hand. They can express emotions and tell stories, and are an important creative outlet for millions of people around the world.

## Melody, rhythm and harmony

The basic building blocks of music are melody, rhythm and harmony. The melody is the main tune. Harmony is when two or more notes are heard at the same time. The rhythm is the pattern the notes are played in.

## Musical instruments

A musical instrument is an object or a device that is designed to be used for playing music. Some are simple, like a recorder, and some are quite complex – a piano can be made up of thousands of pieces! You don't have to use an instrument to play music – you can sing, or use objects around your home to play rhythms on.

There are many different types of dance – from ballets and musicals in theatres to street dance and bopping along to the radio in your kitchen! Dancing can be a serious art form, it can done for fun, or it can be competitive. In the 2024 Paris Olympics, breaking (an urban dance style) was included as an event for the first time.

## Choreography

Dancing that's a staged performance will usually be choreographed. This is when a person called a choreographer will come up with a sequence of moves for the dancers to perform and then teach them the steps.

## Traditional and folk dance

Dance can be an important part of a culture. It can tell stories or legends that are important to a person's heritage, or represent the lives of people from a certain place in the world. The haka is a ceremonial dance of the Māori people of New Zealand. It has been adopted by the New Zealand rugby team, and they perform a haka before each match.

# RELIGIONS AND FESTIVALS

Religion is a set of beliefs that help people find meaning in the world. Religion can include worshipping a god and following teachings and practices that inform how people live their daily lives.

## World religions

There are many different religions around the world. Here are the main ones:

**Christianity** is based around the life and teachings of Jesus. There are over 2 billion Christians worldwide.

**Islam** was founded over 1,000 years ago by the prophet Muhammad. People who follow Islam are called Muslims.

a Christian cathedral

**Hinduism** is thought to have started in India over 3,000 years ago. Hindus believe in a supreme god called Brahman.

**Sikhism** was founded by Guru Nanak over 500 years ago. He was the first of ten gurus that the teachings of Sikhism are based on.

**Judaism** originated in the Middle East around 4,000 years ago and is the religion of Jewish people.

an Islamic mosque

# Holy books

Many religions have their teachings and beliefs set out in a holy book. They describe major figures in a certain religion and guide followers on how to live a good life. Christians have the Bible, Muslims follow the Qur'an, and the Torah is the holy text for Jews.

The Torah is a scroll that is wrapped around wooden handles.

# Religious leaders

Most religions have people who devote their lives to studying the teachings of their faith, such as priests and nuns in Christianity. There are also religious leaders: the Dalai Lama is a leading Buddhist figure, and the Pope is the head of the Catholic Church.

# Festivals

A festival is where people come together to celebrate something significant to them. Some are religious, such as Diwali – the festival of lights. There are also festivals such as Easter, Christmas and the Día de los Muertos (Day of the Dead) in Mexico that have a religious basis but are celebrated by people outside of the faith as well.

pilgrims visiting Lumbini in Nepal

# Pilgrimages

Some religious people go on a pilgrimage. This is a spiritual journey to a holy place. One of the most famous is the Hajj in Islam where every year Muslims travel to the holy city of Mecca in Saudi Arabia. Many Buddhists travel to Lumbini in Nepal, which is the birthplace of Siddhartha Gautama who founded Buddhism.

dressed up for Día de los Muertos

# LANGUAGES

Language is what we use to communicate. Each language is a system that can be made up of spoken sounds, written words and movements. About 7,000 different languages are spoken around the world. Languages grow all the time as meanings change and new words are invented.

## The basics

Words are divided into different groups, such as nouns which are for objects, and verbs which describe actions. Words are combined into sentences to express what we want to say, and use a system called grammar to put the words into the correct order.

## Sign language

Not all language is written or spoken. Sign language is mainly used by people with hearing loss. It uses hand movements and facial expressions to communicate words and sentences. Almost everyone uses gestures to communicate – many people shake their head to mean 'no', nod to mean 'yes' and wave to say 'hello' or 'goodbye'.

Traditionally, Korean words were written and read from top to bottom.

## Writing

In the English language, sentences are written from left to right, but this isn't always the case. Languages such as Arabic, Hebrew and Urdu are read from right to left. Traditional Chinese, Japanese, Vietnamese and Korean texts are written vertically and read from top to bottom.

## Click languages

Click languages use a series of click sounds instead of some letters. Click sounds are regularly used in some African languages and have also been used in an Aboriginal language in Australia.

Mandarin Chinese

**FASCINATING FACT**

The most widely spoken languages in the world include Mandarin Chinese, English, Spanish, Hindi, Arabic, Bengali, Russian, Portuguese, Urdu and French.

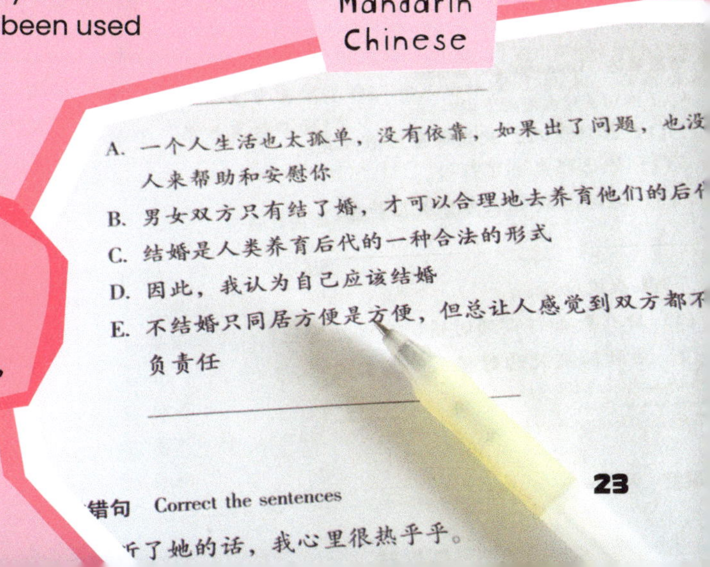

# MONEY

Money has been around for thousands of years, and we use it to buy and pay for things that we need or want. Currency is the money that a country uses – different countries have different currencies, usually in the form of coins and notes. We use currency to give products, food or services a certain value.

## Before money

Before money came along, people used a system called 'bartering'. This involved swapping goods or services with another person. How much something was worth depended on the quality of it and how easily available it was. Anything could be bartered as long as both people were in agreement!

## Coins and notes

Metal was popular as a material to trade, and this was the origin of coins. The first coins were made around 650 BCE in a kingdom called Lydia (now part of Türkiye). The earliest banknotes were called 'flying money' and originated in China during the 7th century.

# Ditch the cash

In 1872, a company called Western Union invented a way of sending money to a different place using something called a telegraphic or wire transfer. People were able to deposit money at a telegraph office. The operator would transmit a message to another office to pay that amount to someone else. Nowadays, less than a tenth of the world's currency exists as money you can hold!

tea brick

cowrie

parmesan cheese wheel

## Alternative money

Lots of things have been used as money over the course of human history. Over 3,500 years ago, the shell of a small marine snail called a 'cowrie' counted as cash. In Italy, wheels of parmesan cheese were used as currency around the year 1200. And in ancient China compressed tea bricks were exchanged.

### TRUE OR FALSE?

It can cost more than the coin is worth to make a coin.

Find out on p.88!

25

# Super Stats

# FOOD

We all need to eat food every day, but our food needs to get to our tables first...

## Five main food groups

Our food can be divided into five main groups.

**CARBOHYDRATES** are where your body gets most of its energy from.

**FRUIT AND VEGETABLES** should make up over a third of the food we eat; they are a good source of vitamins, minerals and fibre.

**PROTEIN** keeps your muscles healthy and helps your body repair itself.

**DAIRY** helps to keep your teeth and bones nice and strong.

**FATS AND SUGARS** should be eaten less often and in small amounts.

### FAMOUS FIGURE: Catherine Nakalembe

Dr Catherine Nakalembe is an expert in agriculture and food security. She uses her knowledge of satellite remote sensing and mapping to improve farming practices by looking at how crops can be made more resilient to climate change.

## Food grown on land

Out of all the land suitable for living on Earth, around 45% is used for farming. And almost four-fifths of that is used for farm animals.

## Food from the oceans

Around 17% of the animal products we eat come from the ocean.

## Vegans and vegetarians

Around one-fifth of the global population is vegetarian, which means they don't eat meat. Around 79 million people are vegans, so don't include dairy in their diet either.

## Food waste

Around the world, about one-third of all food produced gets thrown away. Always try and waste as little as possible!

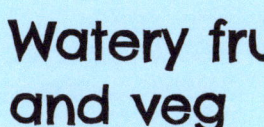

## Watery fruit and veg

Some fruits and vegetables are almost all water! As their name suggests, watermelons are around 92% water, and cucumber is around 95% water.

# Name that...
# WORLD FLAG

Each country has a national flag that represents their nation. How many flags do you know? See how many you can recognise and then check your answers on p.88. Bonus points if you guess the capital city too!

**FASCINATING FACT**

Not all flags are rectangular. Switzerland and the Vatican City have square flags, and the Nepalese flag is made up of two triangles.

# EARTH'S BEGINNINGS

The Earth is around 4.6 billion years old. Before this, the solar system was a huge cloud of gas and dust moving around (orbiting) the Sun. Gravity pulled this swirling cloud together to form larger and larger clumps, which eventually became the planet that we live on and the other planets in the solar system.

## Major moments

**4.6 BILLION YEARS AGO**
The Earth begins to take shape from the clouds of gas and dust.

**4.4 BILLION YEARS AGO**
The oceans begin to form as water vapour in the atmosphere falls as rain.

**4.5 BILLION YEARS AGO**
The Earth's core is formed, and the surface of the Earth cools to form the crust (the bit we live on).

**3.7 BILLION YEARS AGO**
The first signs of life appear as single-cell organisms.

### FASCINATING FACT

The evolution of Earth took billions of years. To more easily understand the length of time, you can think of Earth's history as a single year. On the first day of January, Earth and the Solar System form, animals appear around November-time, dinosaurs are extinct by Boxing Day, and humans appear on New Year's Eve at about 11.35pm!

### 480 MILLION YEARS AGO

With plants to feed on, animals begin to live on the land. The earliest land animal is thought to be a type of millipede, and these were followed by amphibians and reptiles.

### 4.4 MILLION YEARS AGO

Human-like fossilised skeletons have been found that date back millions of years. Humans similar to how we are now gradually evolved.

### 800-700 MILLION YEARS AGO

Sponges (first animals on Earth) begin to evolve in the oceans.

### 2.5 BILLION YEARS AGO

Oxygen begins to build up in the atmosphere.

### 500 MILLION YEARS AGO

The first plants begin to appear.

### 230 MILLION YEARS AGO

Dinosaurs evolved from reptiles. They were the dominant species on Earth before going extinct around 66 million years ago.

# INSIDE EARTH

Earth is made up of solid and liquid layers. When the Earth first formed, it was so hot that it was mostly molten. The heavier parts, such as iron and nickel, which are metals, sank to the centre to form the Earth's core, and the lighter molten rock rose up to form the mantle and the crust.

### FAMOUS FIGURE
### Gladys West

Dr Gladys West was a famous mathematician whose research helped model the shape of planet Earth. Years later, her work led to the creation of GPS (Global Positioning System) which helps people around the world on a daily basis to navigate and figure out where they are.

- crust
- mantle
- outer core
- inner core

## Structure of the Earth

The structure of the Earth is divided into four main parts: the crust (which is made up of tectonic plates), the mantle, the outer core and the inner core.

# Crust

The outermost layer of the Earth is the crust, which is the surface of Earth. It varies in thickness – the crust under the oceans is the thinnest, and the crust underneath the continents is the thickest.

Earth's crust is made up of large, rocky pieces called tectonic plates. The plates move very slowly (at around the same speed that your toenails grow!). Their movement over time means that the continents haven't always been where they are today – in the past, the tectonic plates merged and broke apart to form the continents we know. The areas where tectonic plates meet are called tectonic plate boundaries.

# Mantle

Above the outer core is the mantle. This is the largest layer. The dense rock in the mantle makes up over four-fifths of Earth's volume. The mantle is semi-solid, which means that it is just soft enough to flow very, very slowly.

# Inner core

At the very centre of the Earth is the inner core, which is a solid ball made from iron and nickel. This is the hottest part of the Earth.

# Outer core

Around the inner core is the outer core, which is a liquid layer made of molten (hot liquid) iron and nickel.

## FASCINATING FACT

Have you ever used a magnetic compass and wondered what makes the needle point North? Earth has a magnetic field, and it's the molten iron and nickel that slowly flows through the outer core that creates it. The movement of the outer core means that the magnetic field moves over time. If you were to have used a compass a few hundred thousand years ago, the needle might have pointed South rather than North!

# MOUNTAINS

Mountains are huge features on Earth's surface. They usually have steep sides and tower over the surrounding land. Mountain ranges form along tectonic plate boundaries over millions of years as the plates gradually push into each other, forcing Earth's crust upwards to huge heights.

## Highest mountains

The highest peaks in the world are in the Himalayas, which stretch from Pakistan and through India, Nepal, Tibet and Bhutan. Nine of the highest mountains in the world are in the Himalayas, with more than 100 peaks reaching above 7,300 m. Mount Everest is the highest at 8,848 m.

## Underwater mountains

Not all mountains are on the surface. Seamounts are volcanic mountains that rise up from the sea floor as molten rock slowly erupts and builds up layers of rock over millions of years.

### FASCINATING FACT

A mountain in Hawaii called Mauna Kea rises to 4,207 m above sea level. However, if measured from its base on the sea floor, it's actually 10,205 m high, which is taller than Mount Everest!

## Mid-Ocean Ridge

Underwater mountains are also formed by tectonic plates moving apart. This means the magma can rise up, cool as it reaches the ocean floor, and build up layers that form underwater mountain chains. The longest is the Mid-Ocean Ridge. It's over 65,000 km long, and most of it is submerged beneath the Atlantic Ocean.

Thingvellir, Silfra in the Mid-Atlantic Ridge in Iceland (it is part of the Mid-Ocean Ridge system)

### FASCINATING FACT

As you go higher up a mountain, the air becomes thinner. The air at high altitudes has less oxygen in it than the air at sea level, making it harder to breathe. When mountaineers climb high mountains like Everest, they often take tanks of oxygen with them so that they can breathe more comfortably.

# VOLCANOES

Volcanoes are some of the most spectacular features of Earth's surface. They are openings in the Earth's crust that allow molten rock to erupt along with gases, ash and sometimes solid rock. Molten rock beneath the ground is called magma, and when it erupts onto the Earth's surface, it's called lava.

## Plate boundaries

Most volcanoes are found at plate boundaries. An oceanic plate melts and turns to magma kilometres beneath the surface, and then rises up to erupt as lava. Volcanoes are also found where two plates move apart, which creates a gap for magma to rise to the surface.

## Types of volcano

There are two main types of volcano: stratovolcanoes (or composite volcanoes) and shield volcanoes.

**Stratovolcanoes** are built up of layers of thick, sticky lava and ash, and they have a special steep-sided cone shape.

**Shield volcanoes** form in areas where thinner, runnier lava erupts. The lava flows out over a wide area before it hardens, which creates gentler slopes.

stratovolcano

# Hot spots

Not all volcanoes form at plate boundaries; some form in the middle of a plate. 'Hot spots' are columns of hot rock. The hot rock rises up from the mantle and melts a hole in the tectonic plate so that the magma can ooze out and form a volcano. Over time, hot spots under oceanic plates can create islands as lava builds up and up and eventually reaches above the surface of the ocean. This is how the Hawaiian Islands were formed.

# Eruptions

There are two main ways in which volcanoes erupt: explosive eruptions and effusive eruptions. Explosive eruptions happen when gas bubbles build up in sticky lava. In runny lava, the bubbles simply rise up and pop. But in sticky lava they're trapped, which builds pressure up, until it is suddenly released in a violent explosion. Effusive eruptions happen when runny lava flows more gently onto the Earth's surface, because gas can escape more easily.

effusive eruption of a volcano in Iceland

### FAMOUS FIGURES: Katia and Maurice Krafft

Volcanologists are scientists who study volcanoes, and two of the most well-known are Katia and Maurice Krafft. They dedicated their lives to studying volcanoes up close, often camping out on the slopes to observe and film volcanic activity. Katia's studies led to a greater understanding of eruptions, and Maurice captured spectacular footage of volcanoes in action.

# EARTHQUAKES

An earthquake is when the movement of tectonic plates causes the ground to shake. Most earthquakes are so small they are barely noticed, but bigger quakes can cause lots of damage.

## What causes earthquakes?

Earthquakes happen at points where tectonic plates are sliding past each other or against each other, and become stuck. This causes pressure to build up. When this pressure gets too great there is a sudden snap as the pressure releases and the plates move past each other and go back to their original shape. The snap releases energy which causes the ground to shake.

# Measuring quakes

Earthquakes are measured in two ways: by their magnitude and their intensity. Magnitude is the strength of an earthquake, and measures the amount of energy released. A machine called a seismograph measures this. The intensity measures how much damage is caused by the quake. An earthquake with a magnitude of two is minor, but a quake with a magnitude of eight can cause a lot of damage.

a seismograph

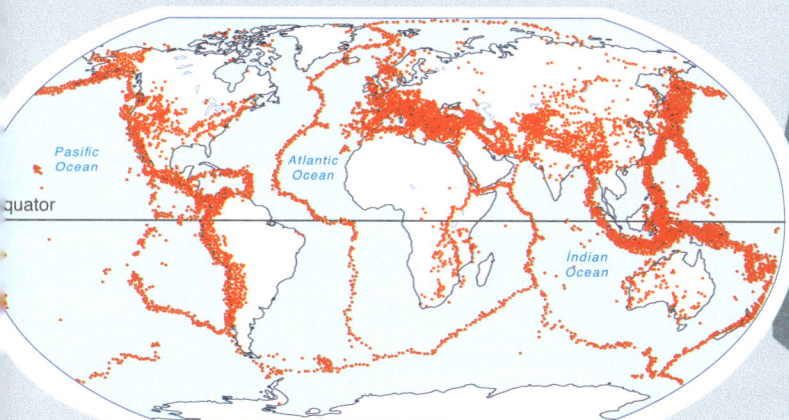

**FASCINATING FACT**

The National Earthquake Information Center in the USA records about 20,000 earthquakes around the world each year, which is about 55 per day. The red dots show all the earthquake zones around the world.

# Staying safe

Scientists still can't predict earthquakes, so they've had to think of ways to keep people as safe as possible when earthquakes do happen. Many buildings in places where earthquakes occur have special foundations and very strong frames that can absorb the shaking. Others are designed to move and sway with the movements caused by the quake, to help keep them upright.

'earthquake-proof' building

# TSUNAMIS

Earthquakes, landslides or volcanic eruptions that happen out at sea can create huge waves called tsunamis that race across the ocean. As they travel towards land they build in height, and cause flooding and destruction when they hit a coastline.

## What causes a tsunami?

Most tsunamis happen when an earthquake causes the sea floor to suddenly lift or drop. This sudden movement makes the water above rise and start spreading outwards. The wave that is created is very long and at the start is quite low in height. As the tsunami reaches the coast, the front of the wave is slowed down but the rear carries on moving, which causes the wave to build higher and higher. The wave then looks like a fast incoming tide and sends water rushing inland.

# High speed

Tsunamis can travel over entire oceans at speeds of up to 800 km/h. In 2011, the tsunami that struck Japan created waves that rushed across the Pacific Ocean for over 9,000 km and broke on the Californian coast only hours later.

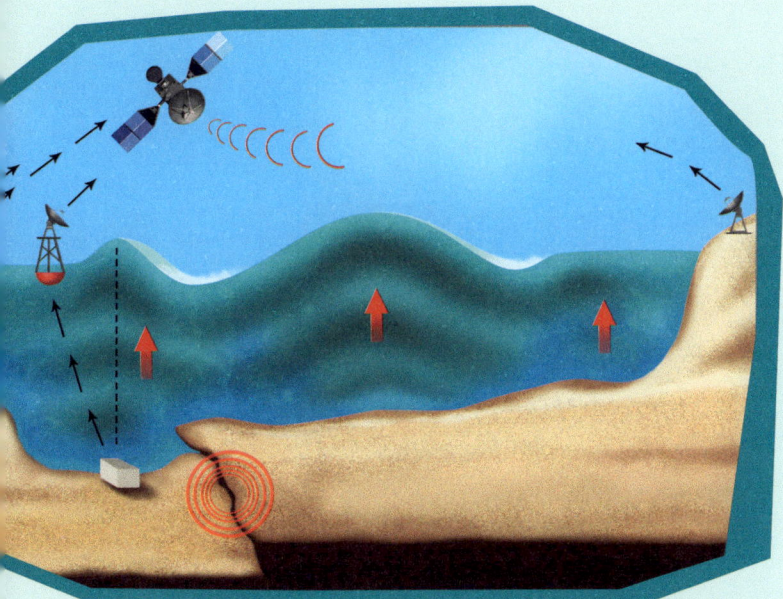

# Early warning

Tsunamis are mostly caused by earthquakes, and so scientists can't predict when they will happen. However, buoys floating in the ocean and sensors on the sea floor can detect them and send out an alert to any areas that may be in a tsunami's path.

**TRUE OR FALSE?** Tsunamis are the same as tidal waves. Find out on p.88!

### FASCINATING FACT

About four out of five tsunamis happen within the 'Ring of Fire' in the Pacific Ocean. This is a horseshoe-shaped string of plate boundaries where there are lots of earthquakes and volcanic eruptions – ideal for triggering tsunamis.

# FOSSILS

Deep inside the rock beneath our feet are the traces and remains of plants and animals that lived millions of years ago. By carefully digging them out, we can learn how life on Earth has evolved.

## What are fossils?

There are two main types of fossil: the preserved remains of a living thing, which is called a body fossil, and evidence of an organism's existence, which is called a trace fossil. Body fossils can include the hard parts of an animal's body such as their bones, teeth and shell. Trace fossils can include nests, footprints and poo!

## Fossil fuels

Oil, coal and natural gas are all fossil fuels. They formed from the remains of living things that were buried millions of years ago. Oil and natural gas formed below the sea beds from tiny marine plants and animals. Coal formed from decomposed trees and plants that sank to the bottom of swamps. Fossil fuels are a finite resource, which means they are either not forming anymore or they are being made extremely slowly – too slow to keep up with what we use.

# How do fossils form?

Fossils form after an animal dies and is buried in sediment, which turns to rock and preserves it.

Trilobites were marine creatures, so when one died it would sink into the sediment on the sea bed.

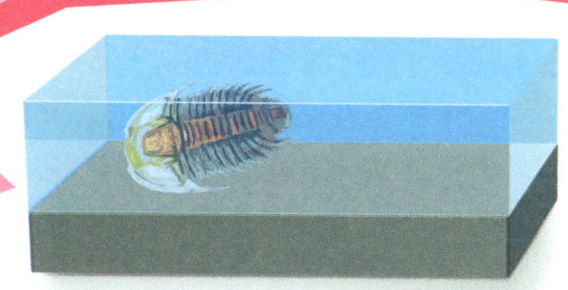

Over time, layers of sediment would build up on top of it as the soft parts of the trilobite decompose. The hard parts, like the skeleton, are left behind.

The sediment hardens into rock. Water gradually seeps through the rock layers and dissolves the hard parts of the trilobite. Minerals in the water replace these and then harden to form the shape of the trilobite.

The rock layers are gradually worn away by weathering, and eventually expose the fossil.

# ROCK

Rock is a naturally occurring substance that is solid and is formed from minerals. It makes up all but the inner layers of Earth, and helps to form the landscape that we see all around us. There are three main types of rock: sedimentary, igneous and metamorphic.

## 1 Sedimentary rock
These rocks form from tiny particles of mud and sand (sediment) that settle in layers, often at the bottom of rivers or oceans. Over time, more and more layers build up and are squeezed together (compacted and cemented) to form rock. Limestone, sandstone and shale are all types of sedimentary rock.

## 2 Igneous rock
These rocks form from molten rock that cools and hardens. Granite, basalt and pumice are all types of igneous rock.

## 3 Metamorphic rock
When a rock that already exists is changed by heat and pressure (but doesn't melt completely), a metamorphic rock is formed. Tectonic plate boundaries are ideal for creating these sorts of conditions. Marble, slate and schist are all types of metamorphic rock.

# The rock cycle

Under the right conditions, any type of rock can become another type. Sedimentary rock can melt and harden into igneous rock, or be heated and compressed just enough to become metamorphic rock. Igneous and metamorphic rock at the surface can be weathered and become layers of sediment that will eventually form sedimentary rock. This constant recycling of rock is called the rock cycle.

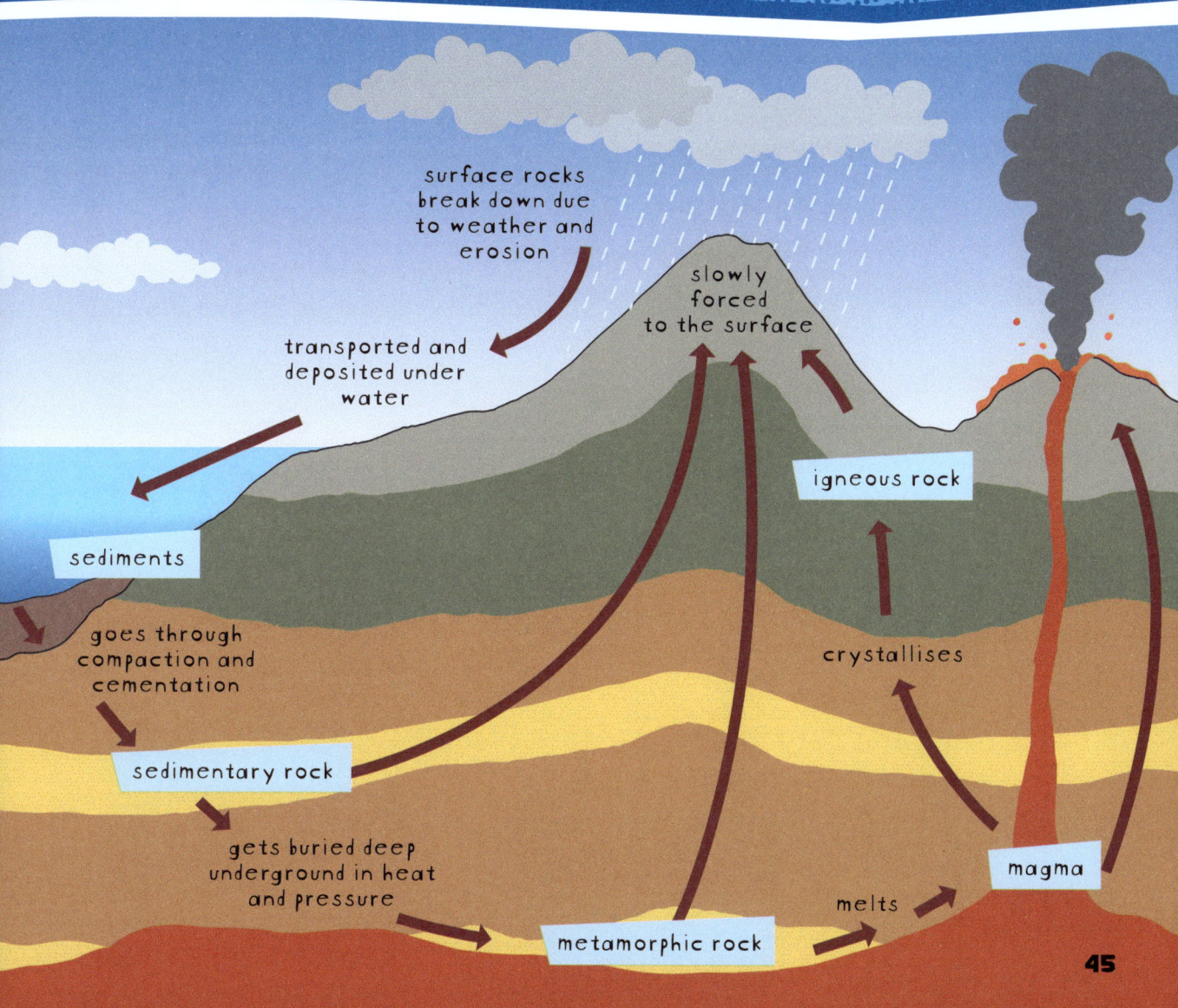

# MINERALS

Minerals are the building blocks of rocks, and each mineral has its own unique chemical and physical characteristics. You'll usually find two or more minerals in a rock, all mixed together from the processes that created the rock.

## How minerals form

Minerals grow naturally in all types of geological environments. Each type of mineral is made up of unique chemicals and is shaped by the conditions it forms in. There are over 6,000 mineral species on Earth and each one tends to have different colours, hardness and textures.

# Geodes

From the outside, geodes look like plain, round(ish) rocks. Inside, however, they are hollow and lined with colourful mineral crystals. Minerals are deposited in the rock by water and slowly crystallise over thousands of years.

stalactites

stalagmites

# Stalagmites and stalactites

Some of the best places to see mineral deposits are in caves, where minerals are deposited by water that drips slowly and constantly. The most well-known mineral formations are stalagmites and stalactites. Stalactites hang down from cave ceilings and stalagmites build upwards from cave floors.

copper ore

gold ore

iron ore

# Ores

Some minerals are more useful and valuable than others, and rocks that contain these minerals are known as ores. Ores that contain metals such as gold, copper and iron are in high demand. Ores are dug up in mines; this process often causes damage to the environment.

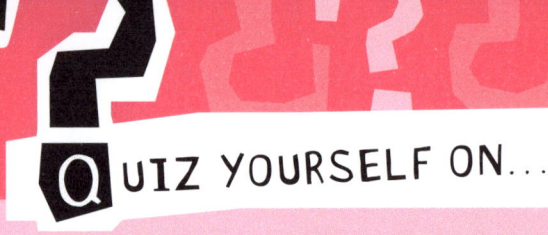

## QUIZ YOURSELF ON...

# PLANET EARTH

It's time to put your knowledge of physical geography to the test!

**1** How old is the Earth?

A. 4.6 billion years

B. 4.6 million years

C. 1 billion years

**2** The inside of the Earth is separated into layers – which layer is directly below the crust?

A. the inner core

B. the mantle

C. the outer core

**3** How many earthquakes happen in the world every day?

A. about 5,500

B. about 550

C. about 55

**4** What are underwater mountains called?

A. seamounts

B. oceanmounts

C. watermounts

Check your answers on p.88!

48

**TRUE OR FALSE?** Europe is the largest continent in the world. *Find out on p.88!*

 **5** There are two main types of volcano. A stratovolcano is one, but what's the other?

**A.** composite

**B.** caldera

**C.** shield

 **6** What is the name of the machine that measures the strength of earthquakes?

**A.** a seismograph

**B.** an earthquake measurer

**C.** a quake sensor

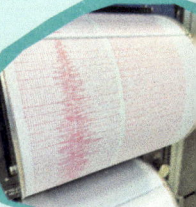

 **7** What is the top speed of a tsunami?

**A.** 80 kilometres per hour

**B.** 800 kilometres per hour

**C.** 500 kilometres per hour

 **8** There are three main types of rock. Which type forms from silt, mud or sand that builds up in layers?

**A.** igneous rock

**B.** metamorphic rock

**C.** sedimentary rock

 **9** Which type of mineral formation hangs down from the roof of a cave?

**A.** a stalagmite

**B.** a stalactite

**C.** a Geode

 **10** What is the hottest part of the Earth's structure?

**A.** the inner core

**B.** the mantle

**C.** the outer core

# WATER

Water is everywhere – in rivers, lakes, oceans, our homes – and it often falls from the sky as rain. We use it for many things in our everyday lives.

## Gas, ice and liquid

Water is made up of the chemical elements hydrogen and oxygen. It can exist in three different states: as a gas, a solid or a liquid. The liquid state is simply water – the stuff that comes out of our taps. The solid state is ice, which forms when water is exposed to temperatures below 0°C. The gas state is water vapour, and it's in the air that we breathe. When it's very cold outside and you see your breath, that's the water vapour condensing into tiny droplets.

**FASCINATING FACT**

Around two-thirds of our freshwater is frozen in ice caps and glaciers!

# The water cycle

The water on Earth is constantly moving through what's known as the water cycle. There are four main stages.

**FASCINATING FACT**
97 per cent of water on Earth is saltwater! The water is salty from rainwater that washes minerals and salts from the land into the sea.

**3 — precipitation**
When enough water has condensed it falls back to Earth as rain, hail or snow. This is called precipitation.

**2 — condensation**
The water vapour rises, cools as it gets higher, and then turns back into water droplets that form clouds. This is called condensation.

**4 — collection**
The precipitation is collected in rivers, lakes and oceans ready to be evaporated again. This is called collection.

**1 — evaporation**
The heat from the Sun warms the water on Earth's surface. The warm water turns from a liquid into water vapour. This process is called evaporation.

# ICE

Ice is frozen water which forms when the temperature drops below 0°C. Ice can cover an entire continent, form a landmass of its own and carve out unique features in the Earth's surface.

## Ice Ages

Way back in the Earth's past there have been periods of time called Ice Ages. This was when global temperatures fell, and ice sheets spread out from the North and South Poles to cover big areas of land – in some cases large parts of continents. The Ice Ages lasted for tens of thousands of years, and there have been at least five major Ice Ages over the course of Earth's history. The warmer times in-between (like the one we're in now) are called 'interglacial periods'.

## Glaciers

Glaciers are huge masses of slow-moving ice that are formed from layers of compressed snow. Alpine glaciers are found in the high mountains and flow through the surrounding terrain, and ice sheets can cover a whole continent.

# Icebergs

When part of a glacier breaks off and floats out into the ocean, it's called an iceberg. You can find them in the North Atlantic, the Arctic and around Antarctica. Icebergs are roughly classified by their shape.

# The Arctic

The Arctic is where you'll find the North Pole, which is the most northerly point on Earth. The North Pole is on a huge piece of drifting sea ice. No one lives at the North Pole, and the closest inhabitants are the people who live in the northernmost parts of Greenland, Canada and Russia.

**TRUE OR FALSE?** Antarctica is a desert. Find out on p.88!

# Antarctica

Unlike the Arctic, Antarctica is a continent because it is a landmass covered in ice rather than being a piece of floating sea ice. It's where you'll find the South Pole. No one lives there permanently, and the scientists who work there only do so for part of the year. The sea ice in Antarctica gets bigger and smaller as the seasons change – in winter, the sea ice freezes and expands outwards from the coast, and in the summer it melts and shrinks.

Penguins live in Antarctica. If you see a polar bear, you're in the Arctic (or at a zoo!).

# RIVERS

Rivers are moving bodies of water that flow through the landscape. They play a vital part in our lives and are home to lots of different plants and animals.

## How rivers form

Most of the water in our rivers comes from rain and melted snow. Lots of small streams and rivers called tributaries flow into the main river. The area of land around the river that is drained by a river and its tributaries is called a drainage basin. A river flows downhill, snaking through the landscape, until it reaches the sea or another large body of water (like a lake). The place where the river meets the sea is called the mouth of the river.

drainage basin

river mouth

tributary

## Largest and longest

The Nile River in Africa is thought to be the longest river in the world. The river flows for around 6,650 km through eleven African nations before emptying into the Mediterranean Sea off the coast of northern Egypt. The Amazon River in South America comes a close second at around 6,400 km, and out of all the world's rivers it has the largest volume of water flowing through it.

## Subterranean rivers

Not all rivers are on the surface – some are underground (or subterranean)! One of the most famous is the Puerto-Princesa in the Philippines in Southeast Asia. The river emerges into the South China Sea after flowing for 8.2 km through a limestone cave system underneath a mountain.

## River economy

Rivers are vital for lots of things in our everyday lives. They can be used for transport, they can be used as irrigation to help grow crops on farms, and they can also be used to generate electricity by having huge dams built across them.

# Super Stats

# LAKES

A lake is a body of water that's surrounded by land. The water in lakes comes from streams, rivers and runoff that's caused by precipitation. Although there are some saltwater lakes, they mainly contain freshwater.

 ## How many are there?

There are over 117 million lakes on Earth! They vary greatly in size – some are smaller than two football pitches.

## The Lake District

How many lakes do you think are in the Lake District? Technically there's just one: Bassenthwaite Lake! There are sixteen bodies of water in the area but fifteen of them have 'mere' or 'water' in their names, instead of 'lake'.

 ## The sea that's really a lake

The biggest lake in the world is the Caspian Sea, which covers roughly 371,000 km$^2$. The Caspian Sea is really a lake because it's surrounded by land, but it's known as a sea because of its size and for political reasons. The five countries that surround it are Russia, Azerbaijan, Iran, Turkmenistan and Kazakhstan.

 ## The highest lake in the world

The highest lake in the world is a crater lake that sits inside a volcano called Ojos del Salado in Chile, South America. The lake is 100 metres in diameter and is at an altitude of around 6,390 m.

## The Great Lakes

There are five Great Lakes in North America: Superior, Michigan, Huron, Erie and Ontario. Around one-fifth of the world's freshwater is in the Great Lakes, and over half of that is in Lake Superior – it's the largest of the five, covering 82,100 km². The Great Lakes can be dangerous to navigate: over 6,000 ships have been lost, with most of the shipwrecks in Lake Michigan.

Lake Superior

## The deepest lake

Lake Baikal holds three world records: it's the deepest lake, the oldest lake and it's the largest freshwater lake by volume. Located in eastern Siberia in Russia, Lake Baikal is around 25 million years old, stretches down to a whopping 1,642 m, and contains one-fifth of the world's freshwater.

## Lakes in Africa

Lake Victoria is the biggest lake in Africa. It covers around 68,870 km² and spreads out over parts of Uganda, Tanzania and Kenya in East Africa. Lake Tanganyika is the longest freshwater lake in the world, running for about 644 kilometres from Burundi down to Zambia.

## The lowest lake in the world

The lowest lake in the world – and the lowest point on Earth – is the Dead Sea, located between Jordan, the West Bank and Israel. It sits about 427 m below sea level and is almost ten times saltier than the ocean.

# OCEANS

Around two-thirds of the planet is covered by oceans. They range from the super-chilly iceberg-filled waters around the North and South Poles to the warm tropical seas at the equator.

## How many oceans are there?

Technically there is one global ocean, as all the bodies of water are connected, but most people recognise that there are five oceans: the Pacific Ocean, the Atlantic Ocean, the Indian Ocean, the Southern Ocean and the Arctic Ocean.

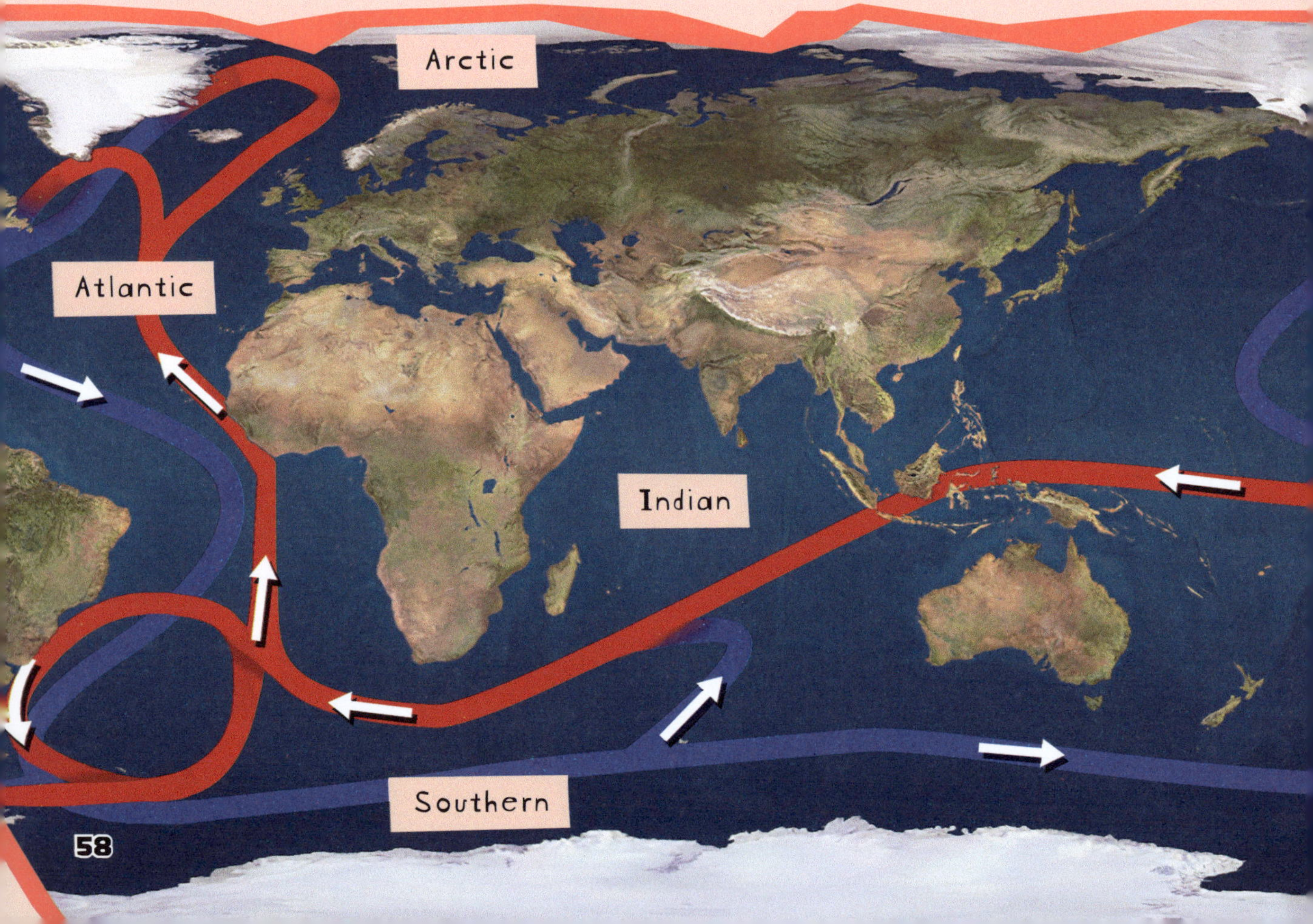

Arctic

Atlantic

Indian

Southern

## Famous Figure: Jacques-Yves Cousteau

Jacques Cousteau was a famous French oceanographer, author, filmmaker and inventor who dedicated his life to exploring the oceans. Cousteau and engineer Émile Gagnan developed the first Aqua-Lung so that people could breathe bottled air underwater and explore the depths for longer periods of time. Cousteau's books and films helped to popularise ocean exploration and gave us a deeper understanding of the world beneath the waves.

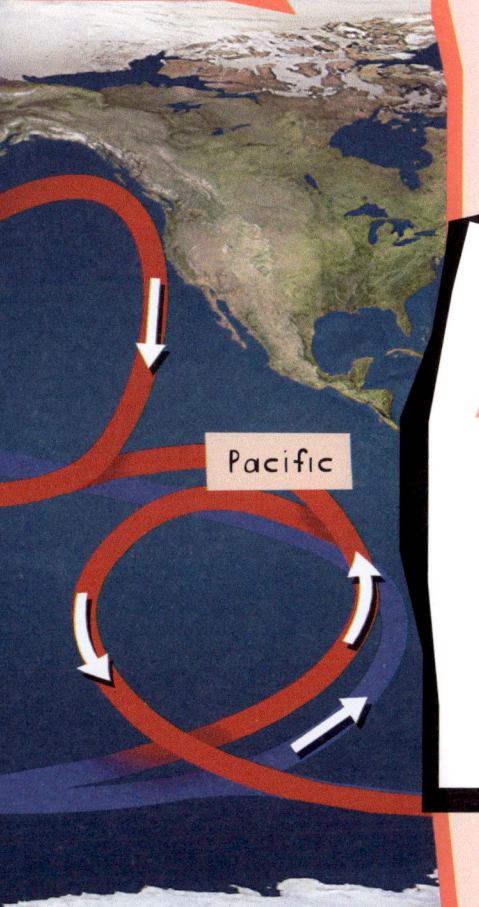

Pacific

# Great Ocean Conveyer

The oceans have surface currents and underwater currents. The currents move cold and warm water to different locations, which changes temperatures around the world. The Great Ocean Conveyor slowly moves a huge amount of water in a large loop around the world, from the northern oceans into the southern oceans and back again.

# DEEP SEA

In some parts of the world, the ocean can be so deep that sunlight can't reach down that far and very few animals live there.

## Ocean zones

As the oceans get deeper, they are classified into five zones:

*Sunlight zone*: the top 200 m of the oceans. Lots of sea life is found here, and it's where you'll find most of the light that's visible beneath the water.

*Twilight zone*: from 200 m to around 1,000 m. The sunlight is very faint but many animals adapt to life here.

*Midnight zone*: from 1,000 m down to 4,000 m. Sunlight can't get down this far, so the only light is made by the highly adapted animals that live there, such as anglerfish.

*Abyssal zone*: from 4,000 m down to 6,000 m. The water temperature is near freezing all the time. Despite this, and the crushing pressure from being so deep, many creatures like giant squid and tubeworms live there.

*Hadal zone*: below 6,000 m. The lowest point in the oceans is Challenger Deep, about 10,998 m down. It is in the Mariana Trench, off the coast of The Philippines.

getting deeper

# Deep dives

Exploring the depths of the oceans is very dangerous: the water is freezing cold and the pressure caused by the weight of the water above is immense. The deepest dive in a submarine was made by Victor Vescovo who reached 10,927 m below the sea's surface at the bottom of the Mariana Trench.

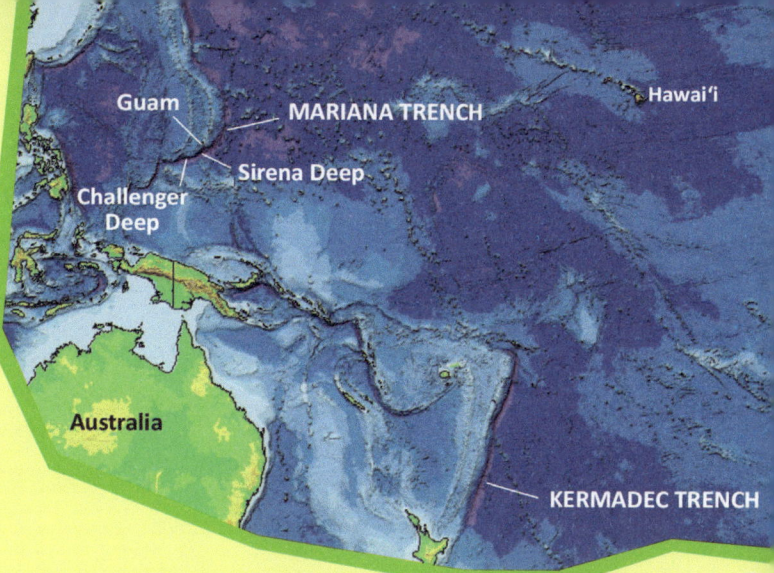

# Hydrothermal vents

In 1977, scientists studying the eastern Pacific noticed that there were deep sea areas where the freezing cold water jumped up in temperature to 400°C! They had discovered hydrothermal vents. These occur when the cold seawater around plate boundaries seeps down through cracks in the oceanic crust. The water is heated by magma and rises back up to create the vents.

# ATMOSPHERE

The atmosphere is the layers of gases that surround the Earth. The atmosphere provides us with the air that we breathe, traps heat to keep us warm, protects us from the Sun's harmful rays, and is where all our weather happens.

## The layers

The atmosphere is made up of five layers, starting with the troposphere and going all the way up into space.

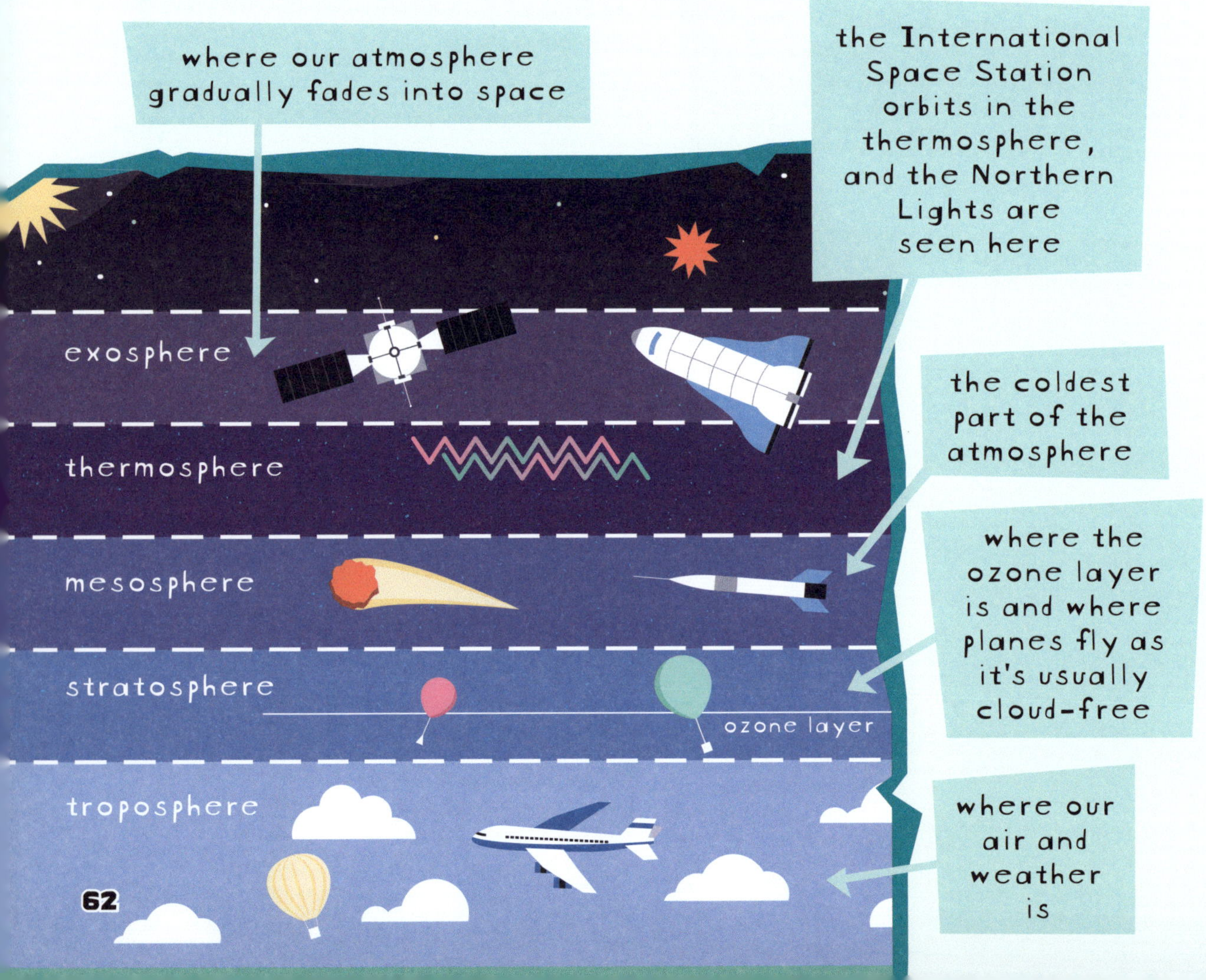

- **exosphere** — where our atmosphere gradually fades into space
- **thermosphere** — the International Space Station orbits in the thermosphere, and the Northern Lights are seen here
- **mesosphere** — the coldest part of the atmosphere
- **stratosphere** — where the ozone layer is and where planes fly as it's usually cloud-free (ozone layer)
- **troposphere** — where our air and weather is

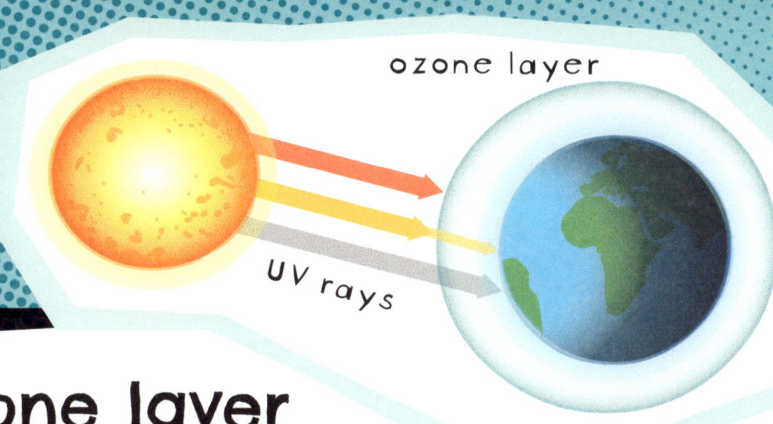

# Ozone layer

The ozone layer is in the stratosphere, and is made of a gas called ozone. The Sun produces ultraviolet (UV) radiation, and while some UV is vital for life to exist on Earth, too much can be harmful. The ozone layer absorbs most of the harmful parts of these UV rays. Some harmful rays do get through, though, which is why people apply suncream in the summer.

# What is air?

Air is the mixture of gases that makes up the troposphere. The main two are nitrogen and oxygen, which make up almost 99 per cent of our air. There are also very small amounts of argon, carbon dioxide, methane, neon and water vapour.

# Climate

Climate is how we refer to the general weather conditions in a region over a long period of time. The atmosphere traps heat, and the movement of the air – along with the movement of the water in the oceans – creates weather. In different parts of the world, this produces different climates, which can be hot, cold, wet, dry and anywhere in between!

# Super Stats

# WEATHER

Weather is the state of the atmosphere in a specific place over a short period of time. It can be rainy, snowy, windy, cold or hot. Weather can be anything from a short spell of gentle drizzle to a raging hurricane.

##  Strongest hurricane

Massive tropical storms that reach a certain strength are either called hurricanes, cyclones or typhoons depending on which ocean they form over. The biggest ever was Typhoon Tip, which happened in October 1979. It lasted for 20 days in the western Pacific, and wind speeds reached 160 miles per hour!

##  Highest number of tornadoes

Tornadoes are violently spinning, funnel-shaped columns of air that form from storm clouds called supercells. They're most frequent in the United States in an area called 'Tornado Alley'. Texas in the south experiences the most, with an average of 136 tornadoes touching down each year.

##  Biggest blizzard

A blizzard is a severe snowstorm. One of the worst ever occurred in 1972 in Iran, where around 8 metres of snow fell during one week.

## Top temperatures

The highest temperature ever recorded was 56.7°C in Death Valley, California in July 1913. Furnace Creek in Death Valley is considered to be the hottest place on Earth, reaching around 46°C or higher during the summer.

The coldest temperature ever recorded was -89.2°C at the Vostok Station, Antarctica in July 1983. In London in 1683 the temperature got down to around -12°C, and for two months the River Thames was completely frozen over.

## Biggest hail stone

It's possible for hail stones to be as big as a golf ball, orange or grapefruit. One of the biggest hail stones ever recorded measured just over 20cm across and fell on the town of Vivian, South Dakota in the USA.

## Most escaped pythons

In 1992, Hurricane Andrew struck southern Florida. It destroyed a facility that was breeding Burmese pythons, and hundreds of the snakes escaped into the Florida Everglades!

# WEATHERING AND EROSION

The Earth's landscape is slowly and continually changing. Plate tectonics can cause these changes, but so can the processes of erosion and weathering.

**FASCINATING FACT**
There are three types of weathering: chemical, biological and physical

## What is weathering and erosion?

Weathering is when rock is broken down into smaller particles by wind, rain, freezing temperatures and temperature changes. Erosion is similar to weathering but also includes the process of transporting the weathered pieces and particles of rock. Both processes work together to shape the landscape.

## Caves

Caves are formed by weathering and erosion. Caves mostly form in limestone, which is dissolved by acidic rain. The minerals from the limestone that are dissolved in the rainwater are deposited and gradually form features called speleothems, like these ones in Jasov in Slovakia.

## The Wave

Sand blown by wind can erode softer rock and create spectacular formations. The Wave, in the Vermilion Cliffs National Monument in Arizona, was initially formed by rainwater running through, but it is now shaped just by wind erosion, producing these smooth waves in the red sandstone.

# DESERTS

Not much grows in deserts, so they are difficult places to live. There are deserts all over the world, and they're not all hot and sandy...

## Hot and cold

Deserts are defined by the small amount of rain or snowfall they get, so they can be hot or cold. Antarctica is the biggest cold desert in the world, and is also the largest desert overall. The Sahara in North Africa is a sub-tropical desert, and is the largest hot desert in the world. In the summer, temperatures can reach over 50°C.

## The Sahara

Unlike Antarctica, where there is no permanent population, there are around 2.5 million people living in the Sahara. Some are nomadic, which means they move from place to place, and some live permanently around oases, which are places in the desert where there is water.

# Desert plants

A number of plants have adapted to survive in the harsh conditions of a desert. The prickly pear cactus has shallow roots to easily soak up rainwater, and any excess water is stored in its pads. Tara trees, in the coastal deserts of Peru and Chile, use their leafy branches to get water from the fog that sweeps in off the Pacific Ocean. In Antarctica there are types of moss that can survive for up to nine months under the snow without water. In the summer, the ice melts so they can thrive and grow.

prickly pear cactus

fennec fox

# Desert animals

Fennec foxes live in the deserts of North Africa. They're nocturnal, which means they sleep during the day to avoid the high temperatures and come out at night to feed. Gila woodpeckers are found in the deserts of Mexico and southwestern USA. They peck out their nests in cactuses rather than trees. Almost all penguins are found in the southern hemisphere, and most live on Antarctica.

### FASCINATING FACT

In the Racetrack Playa area of Death Valley in the USA, rocks move across the bed of the dry lake leaving long trails behind them. They're known as 'sailing stones', and most scientists agree that they move due to a combination of water, wind and ice.

# FORESTS

A forest is a large area of land that is dominated by trees. Forests are found all over the world and are home to many different plants and animals.

## Types of forests

**Tropical forests**, like the Amazon, are found either side of the equator (the imaginary line that wraps around the middle of Earth). Trees here are mainly evergreen, so they keep their leaves for more than one season. Rainforests are some of the oldest ecosystems on the planet.

**Temperate forests** are found in the areas between the cold regions of the North and South Poles and the warmer parts around the equator. They thrive in areas that are not too hot and not too cold, and that have enough rainfall for trees such as oak, maple and elm to grow.

**Boreal forests** are found in the Arctic regions of Canada, Russia, Alaska and Scandinavia. Their pine trees, conifers and spruces can survive the harsh winters and then flourish during short summers.

**TRUE OR FALSE?** Forests help us to breathe. Find out on p.88!

# Forest layers

Forests can be divided into layers – but not all layers are found in all forests. The number of layers depends on the type of forest and the amount of grazing by animals in the forest.

The **emergent layer** is only found in rainforests. This is the top of the very tallest trees. Branches here are unstable, so birds, bats and other animals fly and glide between them.

The **canopy** is a thick layer below the emergent layer. It's where most animals live.

The **understory** is where you'll see smaller and younger trees that haven't reached the canopy. It gets less sunlight and is more sheltered from the wind.

The **forest floor** is covered in leaves and twigs that have fallen from the trees. This all breaks down and the nutrients are released into the soil for tree roots to use as food.

## FASCINATING FACT

In 2012 Dr Julian Bayliss discovered a hidden forest. While researching images of an ancient volcano called Mount Lico in northern Mozambique, he noticed what looked like an undisturbed forest in the crater. Five years later he assembled a team and made the first expedition there to explore it.

# TREES

Trees are all around us. They provide us with fuel, building materials and oxygen, and provide a home for many animals and insects.

## Types of trees

There are thought to be over 65,000 species of tree in the world! There are many different ways to group them, but the most common is to either split them into hardwood trees and softwood trees, or into deciduous (trees that lose their leaves in autumn) and evergreen (trees that keep their green leaves all year round).

*deciduous trees in autumn*

## Bark

Bark is the outer shell of a tree. It can protect the tree from bright sunlight or being dried out by wind. Cracks in the bark provide a home for insects and spiders, and in turn these attract birds. Bark is also a food for local wildlife. Most trees can be identified by the unique characteristics of the bark.

### FASCINATING FACT

Trees can communicate with each other! A complex underground network of roots and fungi lets trees exchange nutrients and send warning signals to each other.

# Leaves

The main purpose of leaves on a tree is to capture energy from sunlight. They do this through a process called photosynthesis. Leaves absorb sunlight along with carbon dioxide and water, using the energy from the light to turn them into glucose (a type of sugar) and oxygen. The glucose is used as food and the oxygen is released into the air for humans to breathe.

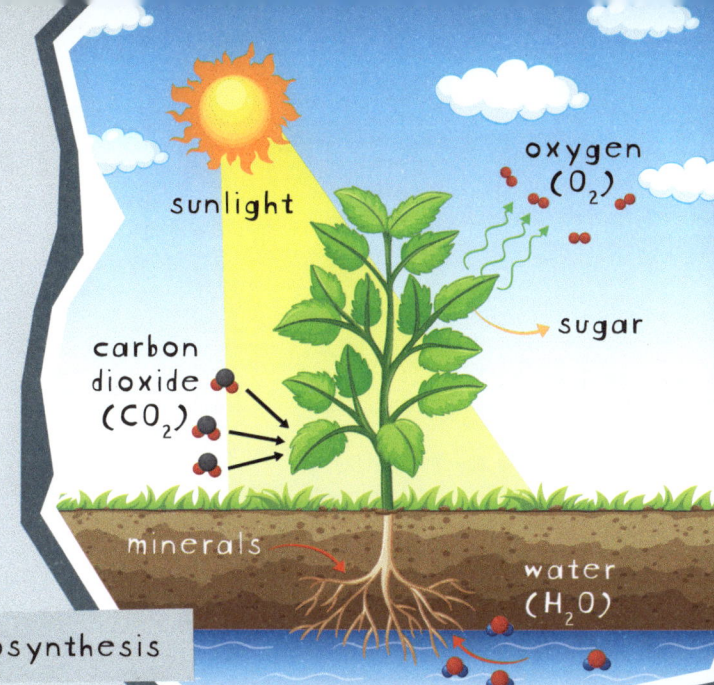

photosynthesis

# Tallest trees in the world

The coast redwoods in the Redwood National Park in California are the tallest trees in the world, sometimes reaching a height of 116 m. They take around 500 years to be fully grown and can live to be over 1,500 years old.

# PLANTS

Plants are living things that grow in the earth or in water. They usually have roots, a stem and leaves. Grasses, moss and vegetables are all plants, and some plants produce brightly coloured flowers.

## Types of plant

It is thought that there are over 400,000 different species of plant in the world. The list is growing too – around 2,000 new types are discovered every year. The most common type is flowering species, which makes up around 90 per cent of all plants.

Venus flytrap

**TRUE OR FALSE?** Some plants eat animals. Find out on p.88!

# Pollination

Most flowering plants need to be pollinated before they can produce seeds. This means that pollen from one flower needs to travel to another. Pollen is a powdery substance produced by the stamen (the male reproductive organ of a flower). When pollen lands on the stigma of the plant it came from, it's known as self-pollination.

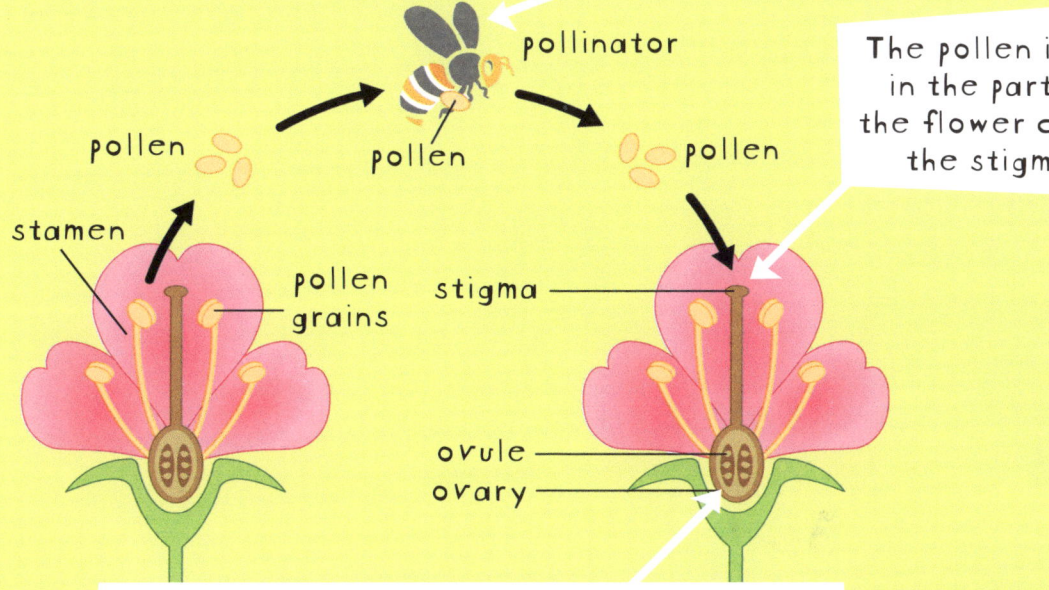

Pollen is transferred between flowers by the wind or by sticking to a flying insect such as a bee.

The pollen is put in the part of the flower called the stigma.

Pollen travels to the ovary where it fertilises egg cells (ovules) to make seeds.

# Germination

Most plants come from seeds, and they need water, soil, oxygen and warmth to grow. Inside the seed, an embryo begins to form, which is like a miniature version of a plant. As the embryo grows larger, it breaks out of its seed 'coat'. Roots grow downwards to absorb water and food from the soil, and shoots grow upwards above the surface to absorb sunlight.

# Name that... FLOWER

See how many flowers you recognise and then check your answers on p.89.

# FUNGI

Although they are often thought of as plants, fungi are more closely related to humans than anything that grows out of the ground! These amazing living things have their own place in the natural world.

## Types of fungi

There are over 155,000 named species of fungi. They can be classified into three main groups: yeasts, moulds and mushrooms. Yeasts are tiny fungi, and they're used for things like baking and making wine. Moulds grow best in moist and humid environments – you'll often find them on gone-off food, but they can also be used to add flavour to cheese. Mushrooms are the most recognisable type – they grow out of the ground.

## Reproduction and growth

Many fungi reproduce by releasing spores into the air. The millions, or even billions, of spores can look like small clouds of dust, and each of them can germinate and grow into a new fungus. They grow underground as a network of threads, and absorb food from material in the soil. Fungi such as mushrooms can also grow above the ground.

The product used to start sourdough bread contains yeast, which is a type of fungi.

# Do NOT pick wild mushrooms!

It takes a lot of skill and experience to identify mushrooms that are safe to eat in the wild. Only a few mushrooms are poisonous but it is easy to get them confused with mushrooms that are safe, so stick to ones that grown-ups buy from the shops.

The most poisonous mushroom in the world is the Death Cap mushroom, which is commonly found in the UK.

**TRUE OR FALSE?**

A fungus is the largest organism in the world.

Find out on p.88!

## Puffballs

Puffballs are large ball-shaped mushrooms that can grow to be bigger than a large grapefruit. Giant puffballs can even be bigger than a football! They don't have an open cap like other mushrooms, and often don't have a stalk or a stem either. Keep an eye out from the end of July to the beginning of November to spot one in the wild.

# CLIMATE CHANGE

Over the billions of years that Earth has existed, the climate has been through massive changes caused by natural processes, from ice ages to sweltering heat. But since the 1800s, our climate has been altered by human activities...

## What is climate change?

Climate change is a shift in temperature and weather patterns over a long period of time, due to human activities. These activities include burning fossil fuels, which pumps harmful greenhouse gases into the atmosphere. Cutting down forests also reduces the Earth's ability to absorb carbon dioxide, so there's more left in the atmosphere.

## Past climates

Scientists who study what the Earth's climate was like in the past are known as paleoclimatologists. They can look for evidence in many different places, for example by drilling into polar ice to find out the levels of carbon dioxide that were present in the atmosphere millions of years ago. By looking at what Earth was like in the past, they can see the influence that humans have had on our climate today.

ice samples used to help research climate change

# The greenhouse effect

Greenhouse gases are gases in the atmosphere that trap heat from the Sun, acting like a blanket to keep Earth at just the right temperature for life to flourish. However, by burning fossil fuels, humans are adding too many greenhouse gases to the atmosphere, which traps more heat and causes the Earth to warm up. This is called 'global warming'.

## Global temperatures

If no significant action is taken to prevent global warming, scientists predict that average global temperatures could rise by as much as 4°C over the next century. This may sound small, but it will lead to more extreme weather, make food harder to grow in some areas, and cause more of our glaciers to melt.

## Coral reef bleaching

bleached coral reef

Warmer seas may sound nice, but increases in ocean temperatures can be very damaging. Oceans have absorbed around 90 per cent of the excess heat caused by global warming, and the wildlife below the waves struggles to adapt. Coral reefs can become 'bleached'. Many types of coral have a special relationship with tiny plant algae that live in the coral. The algae produce about 90% of the food that the coral needs to grow, and give the coral its colour. When sea temperatures rise, the coral feels 'stressed' and expels the algae. This turns the coral white so it looks like it's been bleached. If conditions stay the same, the coral won't let the algae back and it will eventually die.

**Ask an EXPERT about...**

# MARINE CONSERVATION

This is Gabrielle Aisya. She trained in marine conservation and is also a coral planter in Bali. She helps restore coral reefs and teaches people how and why to protect reefs.

### What do you do?

Most days, I go diving to plant corals and find ways to protect them so we don't lose them.

Corals have been here for around 400 million years, but today, almost half of the world's corals are disappearing because of climate change, pollution and human activities.

I help coral pieces attach to rocks and artificial structures so that they can grow into strong, healthy reefs. If I find any problems with corals we've already planted, like coral bleaching or diseases, I try to figure out what's causing it and how we can fix it.

When I'm not underwater, I give talks to locals and tourists in Nusa Penida, Bali, teaching them how to protect coral reefs and oceans. I explain why corals are so important. Coral reefs help protect coastlines, provide homes for marine animals, and even support human life and planet Earth. It's all connected – when we protect coral reefs, we protect the ocean, and when we protect the ocean, we protect our planet.

*Do you have time for anything else?*

**FASCINATING FACT**

Some corals glow in neon colors under blue or ultraviolet light! Scientists discovered that this glow, called biofluorescence, helps protect corals from harmful sunlight and may even act as a 'sunscreen' for the corals. Some fish and sharks can see this glow, but humans need special lights to spot it.

*What does the future look like for marine conservation and coral reefs?*

Scientists and conservationists (like me!) are experimenting and searching for 'super corals' – stronger corals that can survive in warmer waters. If scientists can figure out how super corals are resisting bleaching, we can plant more of them to help reefs survive climate change. Scientists are also looking into coral 'sunscreen' and antibiotic pastes that can be applied to coral reefs to stop bleaching before it gets worse! If these are successful, coral reefs could be protected for many generations to come!

# PROTECTING OUR PLANET

Climate change is very damaging to our planet, but there are lots of things we can do to make a difference and slow down these changes. And some of them are small things that you can do every day.

## What can you do?

You can take simple actions every day to reduce the impact of human activity on the Earth's climate.

### Use less energy
Always turn out lights when you leave a room, and turn off any devices you're not using or that have been left on standby.

### Food
Try to reduce food waste and eat more vegetables. Buying food that's grown nearby will mean that carbon dioxide isn't produced by transporting it long distances.

### Transport
Cars and buses create carbon dioxide, so try to walk or travel by bike as much as you can.

### Recycle and reduce waste
Ask grown-ups to buy products that can be recycled, and try to throw away less rubbish too.

### Plant trees
Trees can absorb carbon, so if there are more trees then more carbon will be removed from the atmosphere.

## Hole in the ozone layer

In the 1970s, scientists discovered that the ozone layer over Antarctica was starting to get thinner. In 1985, a hole was confirmed in the ozone layer using satellite data. Gases called CFCs produced by things like spray cans and fridges were causing the hole, so countries around the world came together and agreed to stop using CFCs. The hole still exists, but the ozone layer is slowly healing now that action has been taken.

### FAMOUS FIGURE: Greta Thunberg

Environmental activist Greta Thunberg began learning about climate change when she was eight. When she was sixteen, she began to take action by calmly sitting outside the Swedish parliament with a sign that read 'School Strike for Climate'. She continues to raise awareness of the effects of climate change and has inspired thousands of people around the world to try and make Earth a greener place.

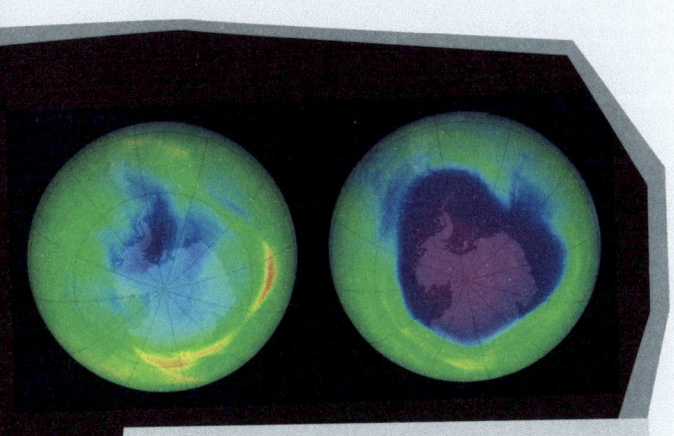

Between 1979 (left) and 2008 (right) the situation in the ozone layer got worse, but luckily the hole is now healing.

## International agreements

Most countries recognise the problems caused by climate change and have signed agreements to reduce the amount of greenhouse gases in the atmosphere.

## Quiz Yourself On...

# OUR WONDERFUL WORLD

Can you beat your score from last time?

**1** What is the biggest lake in the world?

  **A.** the Caspian Sea

  **B.** Lake Superior

  **C.** Lake Victoria

**2** What is the most poisonous mushroom in the world?

  **A.** puffball mushroom

  **B.** honey fungus mushroom

  **C.** death cap mushroom

*Check your answers on p.89!*

**3** What is the deepest part of the oceans called?

  **A.** the abyssal zone

  **B.** the hadal zone

  **C.** the twilight zone

**4** What is the highest layer in the atmosphere?

  **A.** the troposphere

  **B.** the exosphere

  **C.** the stratosphere

**5** What is the name of a violently spinning, funnel-shaped column of air?

A. a cyclone

B. a typhoon

C. a tornado

**6** Which of these is NOT a fossil fuel?

A. natural gas

B. wood

C. oil

**7** Which is the biggest desert in the world?

A. Antarctica

B. the Sahara Desert

C. Death Valley

**8** Which type of forest do you find closest to the North Pole?

A. tropical

B. temperate

C. boreal

**9** How tall is the tallest tree in the world?

A. 118 metres

B. 50 metres

C. 116 metres

**10** What is the name of the process that heats the Earth?

A. the warming effect

B. the radiator effect

C. the greenhouse effect

# ANSWERS

## True or false?

**p.25**: TRUE. It costs more than 1p to make a 1p coin and more than 5p to make a 5p coin, and the price is going up!

**p.41**: FALSE. At one point 'tidal wave' was used to describe a tsunami but they're different things. A tidal wave is a shallow wave caused by the tides that are themselves created by the gravitational pull of the Moon.

**p.49**: FALSE. Asia is actually the largest contient in the world – both by land area and population.

**p.53**: TRUE. A desert is a place that receives little or no rain or snow, and so you can get hot and cold deserts. The snow in Antarctica built up slowly over many years.

**p.70:** TRUE. Forests help us breathe by producing oxygen. Trees remove carbon dioxide from the atmosphere and release oxygen through photosynthesis.

**p.74**: TRUE. The Venus fly trap catches flies and other insects to eat. Pitcher plants have cupped leaves filled with digestive fluid in the hope that insects will fall in.

**p.79**: TRUE. The Armillaria, also known as honey fungus and nicknamed 'the Humongous Fungus', covers just under four square miles in the Malheur National Forest in Oregon, USA. The Armillaria is mostly underground and weighs over 7,500 tonnes.

## Name that...

**pp.28-29: Name that... World flag (capital city in brackets)**

1. Argentina (Buenos Aires)
2. Australia (Canberra)
3. Belgium (Brussels)
4. Brazil (Brasília)
5. Canada (Ottawa)
6. Denmark (Copenhagen)
7. Netherlands (Amsterdam)
8. Jamaica (Kingston)
9. India (New Delhi)
10. Pakistan (Islamabad)
11. Ghana (Accra)
12. Greece (Athens)
13. Japan (Tokyo)
14. Kenya (Nairobi)
15. Nigeria (Abuja)
16. USA (Washington, D.C.)
17. Iceland (Reykjavík)
18. Norway (Oslo)
19. Egypt (Cairo)
20. Saudi Arabia (Riyadh)

**pp.76–77: Name that... Flower**

1. poppy
2. sunflower
3. daisy
4. rose
5. buttercup
6. daffodil
7. marigold
8. lotus
9. lavender
10. carnation
11. orchid
12. iris
13. hyacinth
14. gerbera
15. snapdragon
16. pansy
17. tulip
18. snowdrop
19. bluebell
20. primrose

# Quiz yourself on...

**pp.48–49: Quiz yourself on... Planet Earth**

1. A. 4.6 billion years
2. B. the mantle
3. C. about 55
4. A. seamounts
5. C. shield
6. A. a seismograph
7. B. 800 kilometres per hour
8. C. sedimentary rock
9. B. stalactite
10. A. the inner core

**pp.86–87: Quiz yourself on... Our wonderful world**

1. A. the Caspian Sea
2. C. death cap mushroom
3. B. the hadal zone
4. B. the exosphere
5. C. a tornado
6. B. wood
7. A. Antarctica
8. C. boreal
9. C. 116 metres
10. C. the greenhouse effect

# GLOSSARY

**anthropology** the study of culture

**atmosphere** the layers of gases that surround the Earth

**capital city** usually where a country's government is located

**cartographer** map maker

**city** a very large town that often has millions of people living there

**climate** general weather conditions in a region over a long period of time

**climate change** changes in temperature and weather patterns over a long period of time, due to human activity

**continent** a large geographical region made up of lots of countries

**core** the centre of the Earth – it is split into the inner core (a solid ball made from iron and nickel – the hottest part of the Earth) and the outer core (a liquid layer made of hot liquid iron and nickel)

**crust** the surface of the Earth, which varies in thickness and is split into large, rocky pieces known as tectonic plates

**culture** shared beliefs and activities that give us a feeling of belonging

**currency** the money that a country uses

**desert** an environment where very little rain or snow falls

**earthquake** when the movement of tectonic plates causes the ground to shake

**erosion** similar to weathering, but also includes transporting weathered pieces of rock

Namib desert

Aletsch Glacier in Switzerland

**flag** the symbol or emblem of a country

**forest** a large area of land dominated by trees

**fossil** the preserved remains or traces of a once-living thing

**germination** the process of a seed turning into a plant

**glacier** a huge mass of slow-moving ice that is formed from layers of compressed snow

**greenhouse effect** when there are too many greenhouse gases (gases in the atmosphere that trap heat) trapped in the atmosphere, which causes the Earth to warm up, and leads to global warming

**hydrothermal vent** when cold seawater around plate boundaries seeps down through cracks in the oceanic crust, the water is heated by magma and rises back up to create hydrothermal vents

Buddhist prayer flags in the Himalaya mountains

**language** a system of spoken sounds, written words and movements that is used to communicate

**mantle** above the outer core, it is the largest layer of the Earth; it is semi-solid and is soft enough to flow very slowly

**mountains** huge features on Earth's surface that usually have steep sides and tower over surrounding land

**multicultural** relating to more than one culture

**ozone layer** the layer in the atmosphere that is made of a gas called ozone – it absorbs most of the harmful parts of the Sun's UV rays

**plant** a living thing, usually with roots, a stem and leaves, that grows in the earth or in water

**pollination** when pollen is carried by insects or blown by the wind from one flower to another

**projection** a map that tries to show the curved surface of the Earth on a flat surface

**religion** a set of beliefs that help people find meaning in the world

**rock** a solid naturally-occurring substance formed from minerals

**seismograph** a machine that measures the magnitude of an earthquake

**subterranean river** an underground river

**tectonic plates** large, rocky pieces that make up the Earth's crust and move independently

**tornado** a violently spinning, funnel-shaped column of air that forms from storm clouds called supercells

**tsunami** a huge wave caused by earthquakes, landslides and volcanic eruptions that happen out at sea

**volcano** an opening in the Earth's crust that allows molten rock to erupt along with gases, ash and solid rock

**weathering** when rock is broken down into smaller particles by wind, rain, freezing temperatures and temperature changes

weathering of rock

# INDEX

abyssal zone 60
acidic rain 67
Africa 8, 9
Aisya, Gabrielle 82, 83
Antarctica 8, 9, 53, 68, 69, 85
anthropologist 13
Aqua-Lung 59
Arctic 53
Arctic Ocean 58, 59
art 13–15
Asia 8, 9
Atlantic Ocean 35, 58, 59
atmosphere 62–65, 80, 81, 85
bark 72
bartering 24
bleaching (coral reef) 81–83
blizzard 64
cactus, prickly pear 69
canopy 71
capital city 11
cartographer 8, 9
cash 24, 25
Catherine Nakalembe 26
cave 67
cave painting 13
CFCs 85
Challenger Deep 60
city 10, 11
click language 23
climate 63, 80, 81
climate change 80–83
coal 42

coin 24
collection 51
communication 22, 23
compass 33
condensation 51
continent 8, 9
coral reef 82, 83
coral reef bleaching 81–83
core (Earth) 32, 33
country 8, 9
cowrie 25
crust 32, 33
culture 12, 13
culturual identity 12, 13
currency 24, 25
current 58, 59
cyclone 64
dance 18, 19
deciduous 72
deep sea 60, 61
desert 68, 69
dinosaur 31
drainage basin 54
Earth 30–33
earthquake 38–41
emergent layer 71
environmental activist 85
erosion 45, 66, 67
eruption 36, 37, 40, 41
Europe 8, 9
evaporation 51
Everest, Mount 34
evergreen 70, 72
exosphere 62

farming 27
festival 20, 21
flag 28, 29
flooding 40
flower 75–77
food 26, 27
food group 26
forest 70, 71
forest floor 71
fossil 42, 43
fossil fuel 42, 80, 81
fungi 72, 78, 79
Gabrielle Aisya 82, 83
gas 42
geode 47
germination 75, 78
giant puffball 79
glacier 50, 52, 53, 81
Gladys West 32
Global Positioning System (GPS) 32
global warming 81
globe 8, 9
GPS (Global Positioning System) 32
Great Ocean Conveyor 58, 59
greenhouse effect 81
greenhouse gas 80, 85
Greta Thunberg 85
Gutenberg, Johannes 15
hadal zone 60
hail 65
Himalayas 34
hot spot 37
hurricane 64, 65

hydrothermal vent  61
ice  52, 53
Ice Ages  52
iceberg  53
igneous rock  44, 45
Indian Ocean  58, 59
installation  15
international agreement  85
International Space Station  62
Jacques-Yves Cousteau  59
Johannes Gutenberg  15
Katia Krafft  37
Krafft, Katia  37
Krafft, Maurice  37
lake  50, 51, 56, 57
landslide  40
language  22, 23
lava  36, 37
leaf  73
Lico, Mount  71
literature  14, 15
magma  35–37, 61
mantle  32, 33, 37
map  8, 9
Mariana Trench  60, 61
marine conservation  82, 83
Mauna Kea, Hawaii  35
Maurice Krafft  37
megacity  10
mesosphere  62
metamorphic rock  44, 45
Mid-Ocean Ridge  35
midnight zone  60
mineral  44–47
money  24, 25
mould  78
Mount Everest  34
Mount Lico  71
mountain  34, 35
multicultural  12, 13
mushroom  78, 79
music  13, 18, 19

Nakalembe, Catherine  26
North America  8, 9
North Pole  8, 9
Northern Lights  62
note (money)  24
oasis  68
ocean zones  60
Oceania  8, 9
oceanographer  59
oceans  27, 40, 41, 50, 51, 58, 59, 63, 64, 81–83
oil  42
ore  47
ozone layer  62, 63, 85
Pacific Ocean  41, 58, 59, 61, 64, 69
paleoclimatologist  80
photosynthesis  73
pilgrimage  21
plant  74, 75
plate boundary  36, 37, 44, 61
pollination  75
pollution  82, 83
precipitation  51, 56
prickly pear cactus  69
printing press  15
puffball  79
python  65
rainforest  70
recycle  84
religion  12, 20, 21
Ring of Fire  41
river  50, 51, 54, 55
river mouth  54
rock  42–45
root  72, 74, 75
Sahara  68
sailing stone  69
seamount  34
sediment  43–45
sedimentary rock  44, 45
seismograph  39
shield volcano  36
sign language  22

South America  8, 9
Southern Ocean  58, 59
space  30
speleothem  67
spore  78
sport  13, 16, 17
stalactite  47
stalagmite  47
stratosphere  62, 63
stratovolcano  36
subterranean river  55
Sun  63
sunlight zone  60
supercell  64
Tara tree  69
tectonic plate  32–35, 37–39, 44
thermosphere  62
Thunberg, Greta  85
tornado  64
town  10, 11
tree  70–73, 84
tributary  54
trilobite  43
troposphere  62
tsunami  40, 41
twilight zone  60
typhoon  64
understory  71
UV rays  63
vent (hydrothermal)  61
Vescovo, Victor  61
Victor Vescovo  61
village  10, 11
volcano  36, 37
volcanologist  37
water  50, 51
water cycle  51
Wave, the  67
weather  62–65
weathering  43, 45, 66, 67
West, Gladys  32
writing  23
yeast  78
Zealandia  8, 9